BM

MERCER UNIVERSITY PRESS
1400 Coleman Avenue
Macon, Georgia 31207
www.mupress.org

MUP / H704

FIRST EDITION

Dumas, Carrie M.
Benjamin Elijah Mays : a pictorial life and times
Carrie M. Dumas with Julie Hunter, contributing editor.–1st ed.
p. cm.
Includes bibliographical references and index

ISBN-10: 0-88146-016-8 | ISBN-13: 978-0-88146-016-2
(hardback : alk. paper)
1. Mays, Benjamin E. (Benjamin Elijah), 1894-1984
2. Morehouse College (Atlanta, Ga.)–Presidents–Biography
3. African American educators–United States–Biography.
I. Hunter, Julie.
II. Title.

LC2851.M72D85 2006 | 378.758'231–dc22

2006006615

BENJAMIN ELIJAH MAYS

A Pictorial life and Times

Carrie M. Dumas

with Julie Hunter, contributing editor

Mercer University Press | 2006

Dr. Benjamin E. Mays, December 1980. (Courtesy of Mrs. Ella Gaines Yates)

*This book is dedicated to my beloved
parents, Isaac and Annie Dumas,
who are my role models and
have been my constant supporters.*

THIS BOOK WAS IN THE MAKING MANY YEARS BEFORE Dr. Benjamin E. Mays's death. His persistence in coaching me about the way to go about writing a book made it imperative that I do so.

My deepest gratitude to Julie Hunter for her contributions as my most valued critic. Grateful acknowledgment to the colleges and universities, companies, and individuals for granting permission to use pictures and quotations from their collections. Heartfelt thanks go to the Howard University Moorland-Spingarn Research Center for organizing and preserving the Benjamin E. Mays Collection from which so many of the pictures in this book come. To my friends and colleagues, I am grateful to you for just being there and assuring me that I could do it.

A very special thanks to Dr. Marc A. Jolley, Marsha Luttrell, and other staff at Mercer University Press for their faith in me and in my work.

Deepest gratitude is extended to my family and especially my parents, Isaac and Annie Dumas, for their unwavering support and encouragement. To my sister, Rachel, also a critic, and to my deceased brother, Clarence, who always believed in me.

SAMUEL DuBOIS COOK

THIS EXCITING BOOK IS ABOUT A TRULY EXTRAORDINARY MAN and his unique character, force of personality, achievements, contributions, and noble legacy.

Dr. Benjamin Elijah Mays represented the best of America. He also symbolized and embodied the best of the African-American experience and tradition, the best of the South, and the best of the human condition. His idealism, humanism, warm humanity, and religious faith are as precious as they are rare. The deep beauty of his life and pilgrimage is that they are a constant and dramatic reminder of the higher possibilities of human nature, existence, and destiny.

Perhaps the cardinal lesson of Dr. Mays's magnificent life and rich legacy is deep humility—the profound and compelling recognition of human pretensions (including, or perhaps especially, our own), our inclination to hubris, self-righteousness, moral conceit, self-deception, exaggeration of our own virtues, denial of our own vices, and the tacit assumption that we are the center of reality and that the world of truth, goodness, justice, and beauty revolves around us. The timeless lessons and message of humility are a vital part of his legacy and are deeply rooted in his theology, social philosophy, religious faith, and ethical theory. That we are all men and women, and not God, was a crowning theme of his life and journey. No matter how desperate our efforts, we cannot escape or transcend the harsh, inexorable limitations of our finitude or the fallibility of the human predicament.

Humility, in the context of his vast achievements and phenomenal contributions, was the secret of his greatness. "The destiny of every man is the same," Dr. Mays asserted.[1] "We are born, we live a little while, we get sick or grow old and we die. No time for arrogance and none for pride."[2] He continued, "You cannot help a man if you think you are better than he is. A man may be poor, but don't look down on him. He may be ignorant, but don't take his dignity away."[3]

Sadly, we have yet to come close to an appreciation of the significant contributions of Benjamin Elijah Mays. He was a great human being, a great American, a great Southerner, a great black man, and a great citizen of the commonwealth of humankind.

Of special significance is Dr. Mays's stature as a proud black man. From the perspective of blacks in the American historical process and in the broad sweep of culture, Dr. Mays ranks with Frederick Douglass, W. E. B. DuBois, Booker T. Washington, and Martin Luther King, Jr. in terms of achievements, influence, inspiration, leadership, vision, educational and moral genius, and living legacy. He belongs in rare and exclusive company. Unfortunately, America is far from catching up with the *wisdom de profundis* of Benjamin Elijah Mays in terms of democracy, social justice, race relations, religion, education, pluralism, and human decency.

Dr. Mays was born 1 August 1894, in rural Epworth, South Carolina, the son of former slaves in the nightmarish post-Reconstruction era, "when hope unborn had died."[4] For black people, it was an age of despair and alienation. Rayford W. Logan called the period of 1877–1901 "the nadir."[5] The historical and social context was that of a brutal and heartless environment and culture of celebrated and unmitigated racism, a rigid system of Jim Crow segregation and grave racial disparities, poverty, illiteracy, the dehumanization and degradation of black people, ignorance, misery, lawlessness, massive anti-constitutionalism, mob and other forms of violence, tyranny, Southern vengeance, and Northern retreat, abandonment, and callous indifference.

Benjamin Elijah Mays refused to accept the status and role that history and culture had assigned him. He rebelled. He possessed a superior mind driven by natural curiosity and an intense desire to achieve something worthwhile in his life. Through hard work, great aspirations, determination, preparation, and robust faith in God, he transcended his environment and earned international recognition and fame as a scholar, clergyman, author, public speaker, educator, college president, churchman, public servant, motivator, and transformer of individuals, organizations, and institutions. He became an architect of the Black Revolution, the New South, a more democratic, humane, inclusive, progressive, diverse, and affirmative America, a more equitable educational system, and a more Christian church. Ah, what a rich and noble legacy and challenge for generations and generations to come! Dr. Mays was a seminal figure of the twentieth century.

This book by Carrie M. Dumas is not only rich and fascinating, it is also unique in conceptualization and implementation. The method is to combine the visual and the literary, the photographic and the narrative into a single frame of reference and coherence to depict the remarkable journey and contributions of Dr. Benjamin Elijah Mays. The two techniques are complementary. They illuminate and reinforce one another. The collection of pictures is impressive, with selections from Dr. Mays's birthplace and his college days at Bates to the waning years of his life, when he had lost his legendary vigor. The book is thus pictorial and intellectual, photographic and expository. It deserves a wide audience. Those who knew and loved Dr. Mays will be haunted by nostalgia. They will reminisce and relive fond memories and shared luminous moments with their mentor, benefactor, and friend.

This book is a wonderful addition to the growing body of publications on Dr. Mays. It will not only contribute to a better understanding and appreciation of Dr. Mays's rich life, but also will serve to help celebrate and perpetuate his legacy.

Dr. Samuel DuBois Cook is president emeritus of Dillard University. He is a former student of Dr. Mays.

BM

THIS BOOK WAS CONCEIVED YEARS AGO AS A PHOTOGRAPHIC journal of the life of Dr. Benjamin E. Mays, one of "The Last of The Great Schoolmasters" of the twentieth century.[6] Many people remember Dr. Mays as a great teacher and educator, an eloquent preacher, a spiritual mentor, a molder of minds. His life was the embodiment of his teachings and his wisdom, and his legacy continues to inspire and motivate others.

After fifteen years of close association with Dr. Mays, not only did I learn of his greatness, but I also came to know the many others who were touched by his life and his teaching. Dr. Samuel DuBois Cook, former president of Dillard University in New Orleans, said that Dr. Mays's "genius was as an inspirer and motivator as well as a transformer of young men."[7] In her recent book, *Lanterns: A Memoir of Mentors*, Marian Wright Edelman, graduate of Spelman College and founder of the Children's Defense Fund, characterizes Dr. Mays as:

> A remarkable man and role model for thousands of students who entered Morehouse, Spelman, Atlanta University, Clark and Morris Brown Colleges and The Interdenominational Theological Center that constituted the broader Atlanta University Center of black higher education during his twenty-seven years of service as president of Morehouse College.... Dr. Mays inspired me with a passion for excellence and service....[8]

The Reverend Martin Luther King, Jr. described Mays as "My spiritual mentor and my intellectual father."[9]

Dr. Mays was by no means relegated to Atlanta University Center Schools. At Bates College, where he did his undergraduate studies, the establishment of the Benjamin E. Mays Distinguished Visiting Professorship confirms these basic cultural and academic values—values made manifest in his work and legacy. James F. Orr III of Bates College said, "Mays was one of the most important leaders in society and in higher education."[10]

I met Dr. Mays in 1968 after his retirement from Morehouse College when he ran for (and won) a seat on the Atlanta Board of Education. I was impressed with Dr. Mays's relationship with others, his ability to solve problems, his honesty and integrity in dealing with people and issues. He became my mentor, providing guidance and words of wisdom for my life. Through his encouragement, I saw the wisdom of furthering my education. Through his constant concern, I developed mind, body and soul and understood that they are intertwined. He practiced the presence of God in his life and thereby taught me the spiritual and moral principles of life. Because of this long association, I learned that one's life must be crafted to rise above one's environment with the purpose of contributing to society. Dr. Mays taught me that "Not failure, but low aim is sin." Pushed by such a challenge, I want to share Dr. Benjamin Elijah Mays through this photographic story of his life. It is written to give readers an insight into the power and wisdom of this great giant.

Dr. Mays decided to earn a degree from the University of Chicago when he entered the seventh grade in 1911. He first heard of the University of Chicago from his high school mathematics teacher, Professor N. C. Nix, in the high school department of South Carolina State College in Orangeburg, South Carolina. By the time he reached age seventeen, Mays was still testing his abilities at State College, but it could not prepare him for the challenges he would face attending an all-white institution. The all-Negro student body came from families who were rural, uneducated, and poor, and there was little encouragement for a young African American who desired an education from an all-white school such as the University of Chicago. Still, Dr. Mays admired Professor Nix, and there was no doubt in Mays's mind that he should attend the University of Chicago. It was not until Mays was nineteen that he was able to remain in school more than four months in any year; up to that point, he spent eight months on the farm and four months in school. This had to change if he was to complete his education.

It was then that Dr. Mays decided to take control of his educational path—even if it meant going against the wishes of family. But why was he so obsessed with the University of Chicago? Dr. Mays had always been told that he and the Negro race were inferior to whites, but he never believed it and never accepted it. He set high standards for himself and for those around him. To pursue studies toward a Ph.D. at the prestigious University of Chicago was a lofty ambition. He knew that if he could get his "foot in the door," he could prove that Negroes were not inferior. He wanted to pave the way for the Negro race to show that Negroes, too, possess excellent intellectual capabilities, but often lack the opportunities and resources to develop their abilities and accomplish their goals.

Dr. Mays's long journey to the University of Chicago was not easy. It started in Epworth County, South Carolina, with four months at a county school; five years in the high school division of South Carolina State College, Orangeburg, South Carolina; one year at Virginia Union University, Richmond, Virginia; three years at Bates College, Lewiston, Maine; and finally on 3 January 1921, his dream became a reality, and he entered the University of Chicago to pursue a Master of Arts degree.

When Dr. Mays completed the M.A. degree in 1925 from the University of Chicago, he came to Atlanta to serve as pastor of Shiloh Baptist Church and taught higher mathematics at Morehouse College. After several other positions, which included an appointment as executive secretary of the Tampa, Florida, Urban League in 1926; a post as national student secretary of the YMCA; and an instructor of English at South Carolina State College, Dr. Mays returned to the University of Chicago in 1932 to pursue his Ph.D.

After reaching the University of Chicago, Dr. Mays had difficulty deciding which field to pursue for his Ph.D. degree. He was licensed in 1919 to the ministry and ordained in 1921, but he had also done well in mathematics and philosophy. Eventually, Dr. Mays chose religion, confirming earlier predictions by people who knew him. His pursuit, however, was not without pitfalls. Dr. Mays was faced with racism within the university walls, in the classroom, and especially in social gatherings of students beyond the class. Despite these obstacles, he never strayed from the goal he had set as a seventh grader, and in 1935, the University of Chicago awarded him the Ph.D. degree.

As a result of his many contributions, Dr. Mays has been recognized as one of the great minds of the twentieth century and has left an indelible impression on many of the lives he touched. He received fifty-one honorary degrees, wrote and co-authored eight books, wrote articles for 100 magazines, and contributed chapters in fifteen books. In 1937, Dr. Mays represented the United States at the Oxford Conference on Church, Community and State held at Oxford University (England), and in 1963 he again represented the United States at the state funeral of Pope John XXIII in Rome. He delivered addresses at more than 250 colleges, universities, and schools in the United States and in 1978 was awarded the Distinguished Educator Award by the United States Office of Education, Washington, DC. His portrait was unveiled and placed in the South Carolina State House on 12 July 1980. In addition, Dr. Mays gave wisdom and counsel to many more through his sermons, speeches, and community involvement.

When one thinks of Dr. Mays, one immediately thinks of Morehouse College and the "building of men." He spoke of Morehouse with a passion that gave the impression he was an alumnus; he was dedicated to and truly loved Morehouse. I am reminded of the times I visited Morehouse College and other institutions with Dr. Mays and felt their respect and love for him. Many were in awe of his eloquence in his oratory and in the integrity of his life.

After more than two decades at the helm of Morehouse College, Dr. Mays had yet another goal to fulfill. He often said that many people persuaded him to run for election to the Atlanta Board of Education in 1969. Not only did he win a seat on the board, but also three months later, Dr. Mays was elected president. This position made Dr. Mays the first African-American president in the board's history.

This was a difficult time for the board because it was proceeding with desegregation. Dr. Mays was able to fulfill a role on the board no one else could. His character and commanding presence inspired in those around him the desire to do what was right; he did not need to be nor was he dictatorial. Some felt strongly that Dr. Mays should have insisted—no, demanded—that the board do certain things "now." However, he knew when and how to apply subtle pressures where needed, but he knew when great change was taking place and when and how to let it naturally flow for maximum and lasting results.

In those tumultuous times, feelings ran high, and conflict was constantly in the air, but there was an imaginary line between Dr. Mays and the warring factions in the community, and no one would dare cross it out of respect for him. However upset someone may have been with the events, no one wanted to appear angry at Dr. Mays.

During Dr. Mays's tenure on the board, the first African-American superintendent was hired. Dr. Mays served as a buffer between the superintendent and the community, thereby allowing the superintendent the opportunity to devote his complete attention to the education of the children.

It was my intention when compiling this photographic reflection to instill in generations past and generations not yet born a greater appreciation of the life of Dr. Benjamin Elijah Mays; to show how one man, determined to rise above the circumstances of his birth, accomplished his dreams. I hope that readers will let Dr. Mays's central theme be their inspiration and motivation to greater heights, remembering that "Not failure, but low aim is sin."

Chapter 1

EARLY YEARS

BENJAMIN ELIJAH MAYS, THE YOUNGEST OF EIGHT CHILDREN, was born to Louvenia and Hezekiah, 1 August 1894, in Epworth, South Carolina. He often referred to himself as coming out of his mother's womb kicking. Even though his mother, born the year before the Emancipation Proclamation, could not read nor write, she told him he could be anything he wanted to be. This deeply religious woman brought her children together every evening and often in the morning for prayer.

Mays's oldest sister, Susie, taught him to read before he started to school. Since he was the only one in his first grade class who could read, his teachers predicted that he was destined for great things. His mother valued education and prayed that her son would realize his dream of getting an education. Mays said in his autobiography, "Somehow, I yearned for an education. Many a day I hitched my mule to a tree and went deep into the woods to pray, asking God to make it possible for me to get an education."[11]

Education was the only hope in changing his plight. His church, Mt. Zion Baptist, played an important role in his life by offering encouragement. Through the church, he learned about schools that would provide more education: "My teacher in the one-room school, my pastor, and the church people at Mt. Zion had inspired me to want an education far beyond what the four-month Brickhouse School could offer."[12]

Mays graduated first in his class from the high school department of South Carolina State College in 1916, completing the course requirements in three years. He often commented that he was twenty-one years old when he completed high school. He was admitted as a transfer student to Bates College in Lewiston, Maine, in 1917. Mays heard of Bates College from two of its graduates who taught at Virginia Union University (Richmond, VA) where he attended for a year beginning in September 1916. He was attracted to Bates because of its reputation for debate and because he would have the opportunity to excel as an equal with the other students.

Founded in 1855 as Maine State Seminary, Bates College was renamed in 1863 in honor of Benjamin Bates, an investor from Boston. During his years at Bates, Mays won numerous awards in debate and public speaking and served as president of both the Bates Debating Council and the Bates Forum. He also served as the Class Day speaker during his graduation. In Mays's senior yearbook a colleague wrote, "If you hear him once, you will always remember him."[13]

Mays's mother, a powerful force in his intellectual and emotional development, could not be present at his graduation because the family couldn't afford the trip. Nevertheless, Mays reconciled himself to the fact that these circumstances were beyond her control. However, completing your education and participating in the ceremony meant a lot to Mays. He stated to me upon my completing the master's program at Georgia State University that you do not march for yourself, you march for your family and friends because this is as much their accomplishment as it is yours.

Mays's first job after graduating from Bates College was as a teacher of Mathematics at Morehouse College in September 1921. He made history at Morehouse by teaching the first course in Calculus ever to be given there.[14] He also assumed an additional role in January 1922 as the pastor of Shiloh Baptist Church in Atlanta.[15]

Seventeen years after Mays graduated from Bates College, he was elected to the college's chapter of Phi Beta Kappa. In 1947, the college honored him again with an honorary degree, Doctor of Laws, and in 1982, he was the first recipient of the Alumnus of Merit Award, now known as the Benjamin Elijah Mays Award, the college's highest honor. The Bates College annual intercollegiate debate tournament also bears his name.

Mays said that one of his dreams came true at Bates: "Through competitive experience, I had finally dismissed from my mind for all time the myth of the inherent inferiority of all Negroes and the inherent superiority of all whites...."[16]

(Above) Mays's birth home. (Courtesy of Howard University Moorland-Spingarn Research Center) (Below) Bates College Campus. (Courtesy of the Edmund S. Muskie Archives and Special Collections Library)

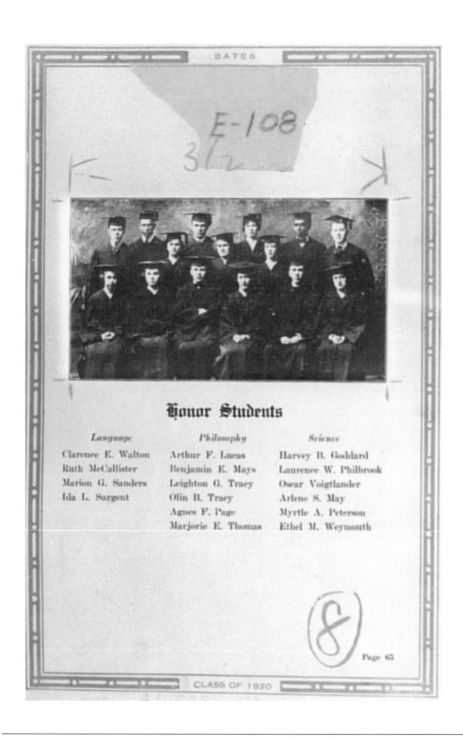

Honor students at Bates College. (Courtesy of Howard University Moorland-Spingarn Research Center)

Mays with 1919 Bates College debate team. (Courtesy of the Edmund S. Muskie Archives and Special Collections Library)

(Above) Mays with Bates College debate team. (Courtesy of Morehouse College)
(Below) Mays with Psi Chapter of Omega Psi Phi Fraternity, 1923. (Courtesy of Howard
University Moorland-Spingarn Research Center)

Twentieth reunion of the class of 1920 from Bates College, June 1940. (Courtesy of the Edmund S. Muskie Archives and Special Collections Library)

Mays with class of 1920 at Bates College. (Courtesy of Howard University Moorland-Spingarn Research Center)

Dr. Benjamin E. Mays and President Thomas Hedley Reynolds of Bates College.
(Courtesy of Morehouse College)

Dr. Benjamin E. Mays speaking at the inauguration of President Thomas Hedley Reynolds, 1967. (Courtesy of the Edmund S. Muskie Archives and Special Collections Library)

Bates College commencement, 1981. Benjamin E. Mays and President Thomas Hedley Reynolds of Bates College. (Courtesy of the Edmund S. Muskie Archives and Special Collections Library)

Bates College commencement, 1981. Benjamin E. Mays, Edmund S. Muskie (class of '36), and President Thomas Hedley Reynolds. Both Mays and Muskie helped present honorary degrees. (Courtesy of the Edmund S. Muskie Archives and Special Collections Library)

Mays with classmate, Mildred Soule, 1982. (Courtesy of the Edmund S. Muskie Archives and Special Collections Library)

Building named for Benjamin E. Mays at Bates College. (Courtesy of the Edmund S. Muskie Archives and Special Collections Library)

Mays after receiving the Bates College Alumnus Merit Award. (Courtesy of Morehouse College Archives)

Mays at his sixtieth class reunion from Bates, 1980. (Courtesy of the Edmund S. Muskie Archives and Special Collections Library)

Chapter 2

THE HOWARD YEARS, 1934–1940

BENJAMIN MAYS SAW HOWARD UNIVERSITY FOR THE FIRST time in 1926, the year Mordecai Johnson, Howard's first African-American president, was elected. Dr. Mays was attracted to Howard because of his admiration for Johnson, but it was Channing Tobias, a leader with the YMCA, who knew Mays when he was a high school student at South Carolina State College and recommended him to President Johnson for the deanship of the School of Religion. Dr. Mays wanted to make the School of Religion outstanding, to elevate it from its stepchild position to a place of respectability at the institution. President Johnson named Mays the second black dean of the School of Religion in 1934.[17]

Mays immediately identified an ambitious agenda to address the needs of the School of Religion: (1) to increase the enrollment (only twenty-eight students were enrolled); (2) to improve the faculty; (3) to rehabilitate the physical plant; (4) to enlarge and improve the library; (5) to establish an endowment; and (6) to seek accreditation by the American Association of Theological Schools.

In his six-year tenure, Mays met four of the goals. Enrollment had increased to forty-three college students pursuing either a B.D. degree or an M.A. in Religion Education. The school had developed a good recruiting program; and the following year fifty-three students, all college graduates, were enrolled. This dramatic increase in enrollment must be attributed to recruitment and to a group of able teachers.[18]

Mays also managed to strengthen the faculty. Perhaps the most important factor in building a theological school restricted to college graduates was the number of Negro teachers who were well known nationally in the Negro community such as Bishop William Y. Bell, J. Leonard Farmer, William Stuart Nelson, and Howard W. Thurman.

However, with the library Mays surpassed his expectations and met his fourth goal: improving the library. Auburn Theological Seminary in New

York was merging with Union Theological Seminary (also in New York) and was asking $10,000 for the 39,000 books in its Auburn's library. Mays convinced President Johnson that the books were worth the considerable price. The collection, which dated back to the 1900s, consisted of a broad selection of resources to support the divinity school's curriculum and the scholarship of its faculty. According to Leonard Teel's article, Mays said, "I was able to show President Johnson that at the annual rate we were buying books, it would take the School of Religion seventy-five years to purchase 39,000 volumes. Such persuasion, pressure, and persistence is the duty of every dean and every chairman of a department if he wants to get things done."

Mays was also concerned with the image of the Divinity School and felt that the physical facility did nothing to raise its level of prominence. When the School acquired the Carnegie library building on the main campus, Mays felt that not only was the school moving up, but that the faculty could be strengthened and morale heightened.

Mays is also credited with shepherding the School of Religion through its initial accreditation process in the American Association of Theological Schools in 1939. This was accomplished with its better appointed library, its richer curriculum, its better prepared student body and with its well-trained faculty, the School of Religion has since 1932, working in cooperation with the Graduate School, offered work leading to the Master of Arts degree in Religious Education. This curriculum is organized to make it possible for a person without a B.D. degree to complete his work leading to the M.A. degree in two years. The first year of such study is devoted almost entirely to religious fields which are related to but lie outside of religious education. The second year is given to intensive study and research within the field of Religious Education itself.

Prior to 1934, the School of Religion was an institution for graduating men with the Bachelor of Theology degree. This required only two years of college and two years of theological training. The B.Th. degree was phased out in 1934 with the goal of making the School of Religion a full-fledged professional school, accepting only college graduates and offering higher degrees.[19]

Because Mays achieved all but two of the needs on his list—the endowment and the physical plant—his six-year tenure (1934–1940) at the School of Religion was a turning point in the life of the school, according to Dr. Lawrence N. Jones, former dean of the School of Divinity at Howard. Funds for any kind of major endeavor were scarce, so the endowment and the physical plant took a backseat to the other needs.

The Howard University Graduate Council voted on 13 October 1936 to approve Dean Mays's request that the Department of Religious Education be permitted to offer a major, leading to the degree of Master of Arts. Thus, in 1937, the first Master of Arts Degree in Religious Education was awarded to two students—Anita Turpean Anderson and Alfonso J. Edwards.

While at Howard University, Mays represented the United States at various world conferences; namely, the YMCA of America at plenary sessions of the World Committee, Stockholm, Sweden, 1938; the United States at Oxford Conference on Church, Community and State, Oxford University, England, 1937; and Leader in Youth Conference, Amsterdam, Holland, 1939. Mays, with twelve other Americans, attended the World Conference of the YMCA in Mysore, India, in 1937.

After leaving Howard in 1940, Mays was invited fourteen times to deliver sermons in Rankin Chapel on Howard's campus. His sermon titles alone motivated pre-discussions and anticipation. Some of these titles included the following: "The Great Desire and How to Attain It"; "How Important is Happiness?"; "How Adequate is Your God?"; "Man's Dependence Upon God and His Quest for Immortality"; "How Righteous Is Your Righteousness?"; "We Serve Man By Serving God"; "Religion Promises No Bed of Roses"; "Beyond Ur of the Chaldees Lies Canaan"; "Martyrs and Their Contribution to Humanity"; and "Genesis or Evolution, Which?"[20]

These sermons are just as relevant today as they were when they were delivered. This demand for him as a speaker, preacher, lecturer, thinker, leader was felt throughout the life and times of Dr. Mays.

Over the years, Howard University School of Divinity has honored Dr. Mays's vital role in the history of the institution. In 1987, the new home of the School of Divinity was officially named the Benjamin E. Mays Hall. It is located on twenty-two pastoral acres, and its approximately 110,000 square feet include a library, classrooms, offices, dormitory, and recreational space.

Andrew Rankin Memorial Chapel, Howard University, Washington, DC. (Courtesy of Howard University Moorland-Spingarn Research Center)

Choir marching into Rankin Memorial Chapel, Howard University. (Courtesy of Howard University Moorland-Spingarn Research Center)

Dean Mays and students of the Howard University School of Religion, ca. 1939–1940. (Courtesy of Howard University Moorland-Spingarn Research Center)

Dr. Mays and former presidents of Howard University: Dr. James Cheek, Dr. Mordecai Johnson, and Dr. James Nabrit. Far right is Dr. Michael R. Winston of Howard's Moorland-Spingarn Research Center. 1967. (Courtesy of Howard University Moorland-Spingarn Research Center)

Benjamin E. Mays Hall at Howard University School of Divinity.
(Courtesy of Sherri Fillingham, communications assistant to the dean)

Chapter 3

MOREHOUSE COLLEGE YEARS, 1940–1967

ON 1 JULY 1940, DR. BENJAMIN E. MAYS BECAME THE SIXTH president of Morehouse College, an all-male liberal arts institution in Atlanta, Georgia. Morehouse had given Mays his first teaching position in the early twenties and had now chosen him to head the institution. Morehouse, a Baptist-affiliated institution, was founded in 1867 in the basement of Springfield Baptist Church in Augusta, Georgia, and was first known as Augusta Institute. Mays spent twenty-seven years as president of Morehouse College, a period that is chronicled as the "keystone of his career as a great educator, theologian and leader of his people."[21]

In 1940, when Mays accepted this position, the morale at Morehouse was at an all-time low among faculty, staff, students, and alumni. In his last commencement address before retiring, Mays depicted 1940 as a period of naked racism that permeated this institution and all other institutions responsible for training the minds of young black leaders. Faced with a societal philosophy which clouded any achievement of success and professed that Negroes were untrainable, "shiftless, inferior to whites, and possess no love and no hope for a better future,"[22] Mays confronted a Morehouse College that was the weakest link among the affiliated institutions in the Atlanta University System—the physical plant was inadequate, the faculty continued to decrease, the endowment was small, and World War II would soon deplete its all-male student body.[23]

Undaunted, Mays decided this challenge was not set before him to fail. He believed that Morehouse College must prove that Negroes possessed a high level of intelligence and that training was the missing factor. Hence, his first priority was to identify the immediate needs of the college and to set an agenda to address the timeline for accomplishing each need. Soon after Mays developed his plan, World War II began and dramatically constrained the college's ability to continue since more students were being drafted. The picture was so bleak that the chairman of the Morehouse Board of Trustees approached Mays with a recommendation to close the college for the duration of the war. Mays's response was an emphatic "Not on your life! Not on your life! Because if Morehouse closes, it'll never open its doors again."[24]

Believing that the strength of the Atlanta University system was drawn from the strength of each of its components and that the weakness of any one of its components weakened the whole system, Mays set about to strengthen Morehouse College, to make Morehouse equal to its partnering institutions. He proposed to the board chairman that Morehouse College market its program to males fourteen and fifteen years old—too young to be drafted into the armed services, but not too young to be trained. Mays later said of that proposal, "We put together our own tests and went throughout the country asking for the fourteen-year-old students. That's how I found Martin Luther King, Jr. I found him because I was trying to save Morehouse from being closed."[25]

Immediately, the morale improved and the "Morehouse spirit began to hum."[26] The second move Mays made was to improve the academic quality of the student body. Because of the gradual increase in the enrollment beyond 1941, the faculty made monumental strides in training the whole student: mind, body, and soul. It was never strange to find a Morehouse professor teaching and conversing with the Morehouse student on the campus. Professors weren't only interested in teaching their curriculum; they sought to pass on to students social graces, how to dress, how to speak correctly, how to show respect. In addition, these informal conversations provided the opportunity for students to discuss major concepts heard during class lectures or other issues that arose during the learning process. These events directly point to the school's philosophical goals and objectives: "To improve the quality and the quantity of the program to the end that graduates will improve the quality and quantity of their leadership in their respective communities."[27]

In the twenty-seven years during Mays's leadership, the enrollment increased 169 percent, from 358 to 962 students. Likewise, there was considerable motivation on the part of these graduates to further their training by enrolling in graduate and professional schools to receive higher degrees. In his summation of the years of leadership at Morehouse, Mays reported that "of the 118 Morehouse graduates who have earned the Ph.D. degree, 52 (44 percent) of them graduated from Morehouse since 1943, representing thirty-four universities. "Although the majority of our graduates entering medical schools go to Meharry and Howard," Mays reported, "increasing numbers are being admitted to medical schools like the University of Chicago, Western Reserve, Rochester, Harvard, Emory, Boston and the University of Texas."[28] This has always been a pride of Morehouse College and justifies the "Morehouse Mystique."[29]

Mays's third move was to improve the quality of the faculty. While this was done simultaneously with improving the quality of the student body, it was Mays's philosophy that "not to provide the students with the ablest faculty available is criminal and irresponsible."[30] The faculty went from twenty-three full time members in 1940 to sixty-five in 1966–1967. In 1940, two full-time teachers had earned the Ph.D. and in 1966–1967, thirty-four (52.3 percent) held doctorates.[31]

To challenge the minds of the student body, Dr. Mays lectured at "Tuesday Morning Chapel" in historic Sale Hall, where students learned about the black church and where he challenged and inspired them to excel in scholarship and in life itself.

Several of Dr. Mays's books including *The Negro Church*, (with Joseph Nicholson), *The Negro God, Seeking to Be Christian in Race Relations, A Gospel for The Social Awakening*, and a pamphlet entitled " The Christian in Race Relations" served as excellent resources for his lectures. Many Morehouse men speak highly of Dr. Mays's sermons in which he frequently spoke about stewardship, responsibility, and engagement. Mays said that the students would approach him after chapel and want to chat and ask questions. He said, "They came first in my book. Sadie and I often had them over to the house just to sit and chat. That was good too. We all learned a lot."[32] A phrase often used by Morehouse graduates is that "Mays was a builder of men" through these kinds of programs.

Tuesday was the president's day at chapel, and he usually spoke to students or had charge of the service. Chapel was compulsory for the students. Mays said that even though students were required to attend chapel, he has met no former students who do not look back on the Morehouse Chapel as a place where they received something valuable that they would not have gotten elsewhere. The chapel remained for twenty-five years of Mays's presidency.[33]

Dr. Clinton Warner, a freshman during Mays's first year as president, recalls one of Mays's sermons vividly:

He stated a freshmen from Mars would likely be appalled and horrified at the attitude of students that I see everyday—bad study habits, no interest in learning, time spent having a good time, cutting classes and just laziness.

Subsequently, he gave inspiring reasons why we all should be proud of ourselves and strive to do the best job that we could—at Morehouse and in the world. Mays advised, "Whatever you do, strive to do it so well that no man living and no man dead and no man yet to be born could do it any better."[34] If this advice did not create the "Morehouse Mystique," it certainly enhanced it.

To Dr. Mays, academic preparation also included international travel. During his tenure, the Merrill Travel Study Award was instituted in 1954 by educator and philanthropist, Charles Merrill, who later became chairman of the Morehouse Board of Trustees. The travel study award enabled students to study and travel in Europe for a year and enabled faculty to study for a summer. Mr. Merrill said in a Morehouse chapel program in 1958 that "he had gained as much as the recipients of the grant from the experience of giving and helping others to extend their cultural horizons and to improve their education."[35] The Merrill Travel Study program continues to provide global experiences for Morehouse students today. Morehouse is fortunate to have had a visionary with a global perspective of education.[36]

Dr. Mays encouraged his students to travel beyond their backyards, to look beyond America's racism and segregation, and to prepare for equality and justice. Consequently, Dr. Mays's vision and encouragement heightened the self-esteem of the "Morehouse Man." Dr. Mays not only talked about excellence in chapel, but he also demonstrated it in his lifestyle. He was a role model for the students, faculty, and staff. Dr. Mays once said, "I spent half of my life demonstrating to myself that I was not inferior; I spent the rest carrying that message to the students at Morehouse."[37]

Charlie Moreland, Morehouse class of 1951, vividly remembers Dr. Mays stressing the importance of academic preparation. He recalls that Dr. Mays often said that, "if someone is looking for a person to do a job in your field, you should be so well prepared, he would have to choose you for the job."[38]

As a visionary and administrator, Mays was often ahead of his time. He understood the need for a larger endowment and higher salaries for the faculty. Dr. Mays earned the nickname, "Buck Bennie," because of his strict business mind and financial emphasis. According to Dr. Clinton Warner, Dr. Mays realized that his aspirations for Morehouse could only be obtained through sound economic backing.

Dr. Mays often remarked, "I realized that God had called me to do something worthwhile in the world" (See chapter 5 for the full quote.). According to Mr. Charles Merrill, that strength of religious faith, that very evident conviction behind his words— "The birthright of equality is given by God"—that moral integrity behind his reserved courtesy made it difficult for anyone to push Dr. Mays around. History will honor and document Dr. Mays's contributions to the world.

Morehouse College bestowed a lasting honor upon Dr. Mays when it selected a space on its campus to be the final resting place for him and his beloved wife, Sadie. On this spot was also erected a life-sized statue of Dr. Mays.

Benjamin E. Mays at his desk at Morehouse College.
(Courtesy of Howard University Moorland-Spingarn Research Center)

Dr. Benjamin E. Mays and President Florence Matilda Read, president of Spelman College, 1942. (Courtesy of Howard University Moorland-Spingarn Research Center)

Dr. Benjamin E. Mays and President Florence Matilda Read of Spelman College.
(Courtesy of Morehouse College)

Seventy-fifth anniversary celebration of Morehouse College. Dr. Mays, J. W. Dobbs, Mrs. Kemper Harreld, Dr. L. O. Lewis. (Courtesy of Howard University Moorland-Spingarn Research Center)

United Negro College Fund Meeting, California, 1949. (Courtesy of Spelman College Archives)

Mays with United Negro College Fund presidents, 1954: Dr. Albert Manley, Spellman College; Dr. Matthew S. Davage, Huston-Tillotson; Dr. Rufus Clement, Atlanta University; Dr. W. R. Strassner, Shaw University; Dr. J. S. Scott, Sr., Wiley College; Dr. Charles Johnson, Fisk University; Mr. William Trent, Jr., executive director, UNCF; Dr. Chester Kirkendoll, Lane College; Dr. Richard V. Moore, Bethune-Cookman College; Dr. Harold Trigg, St. Augustine College; Dr. Edmund Peters, Paine College. (Courtesy of Spelman College Archives)

Mays attending meeting of UNCF presidents in New York, 1955. (Courtesy of Spelman College Archives)

Mays featured with other ministers at the Ministers Institute, Morehouse College, July 1947. Seventy-eight ministers and church workers were enrolled in the Third Annual Baptist Ministers Institute. (Courtesy of Spelman College Archives)

Atlanta University Center presidents at 1947 commencement: F. B. Washington, Dr. Rufus Clement, Miss Florence Read, Mr. Seltzer, D. W. H. McKinney, and Dr. Benjamin E. Mays. (Courtesy of Spelman College Archives)

Mays featured with President Rufus Clement of Atlanta University, President Florence Read of Spelman College, President Harry V. Richardson of Gammon Theological Seminary, President James P. Brawley of Clark College, and President John H. Lewis of Morris Brown College. (Courtesy of Spelman College Archives)

Platform party for 1948 Atlanta University commencement: Dr. Rufus Clement, Dr. John W. Davis, Miss Florence Read, and Dr. Benjamin E. Mays. (Courtesy of Spelman College Archives)

Atlanta University Center presidents and speakers at commencement, June 4, 1951:
Rev. Robert Buchanan Giffen, Mr. Solomon W. Walker, Dr. Roger Philip McCutcheon,
Dean J. Gordon Stipe, Miss Florence Read, Dr. Benjamin E. Mays, and Rev. Homer Clyde
McEwen. (Courtesy of Spelman College Archives)

Platform party for Atlanta University Center commencement, 1952: Rev. Lucius Miles, Providence Baptist Church; President Rufus Clement, Atlanta University; President Benjamin E. Mays, Morehouse College; President Albert W. Dent, Dillard University; Rev. Dennis C. Washington, Seventeenth Street Baptist Church, Anniston, Alabama; President Florence Read, Spelman College; and Rev. Sam T. Cobb, rector of Holy Innocents' Episcopal Church. (Courtesy of Spelman College Archives)

The Atlanta University Convocation presidents and guest, 29 January 1956: Dr. Benjamin
E. Mays, Dr. James Brawley, Dr. Albert Manley, Dr. Graham, Dr. Rufus Clement, Dr. Harry
Richardson, and Dr. John H. Lewis. (Courtesy of Spelman College Archives)

Platform party for the 8 June 1953, Spelman College commencement, Sisters Chapel:
Dr. Rufus Clement, Dr. Lewis M. Hammond, Miss Florence Read, and Dr. Benjamin E.
Mays.
(Courtesy of Spelman College Archives)

Dr. Albert Manley of Spelman College, Dr. Martha B. Lucas and Dr. Benjamin E. Mays. (Courtesy of Spelman College Archives)

1964 Spelman College Commencement platform party: Mrs. Grace Perry, Rev. Robert J. McMullen, Rev. Norman Rates, Dr. Benjamin E. Mays, Dr. Mabel M. Smythe, Dr. Albert Manley, Dr. Oran Eagleson, Dr. Rufus Clement, and Rev. Adolphus Dickerson. (Courtesy of Spelman College Archives)

Dr. Rufus Clement, Dr. Benjamin E. Mays, Congressman John Brademas, and commencement speaker at Spelman College Dr. Albert Manley. (Courtesy of Spelman College Archives)

Dr. Benjamin E. Mays, Mattiwilda Dobbs, and Dr. Albert Manley. (Courtesy of Howard University Moorland-Spingarn Research Center)

Dr. Benjamin E. Mays with distinguished lady. (Courtesy of Howard University Moorland-Spingarn Research Center)

Dr. Mays poses with the men of Alpha Rho Chapter of Alpha Phi Alpha Fraternity, May 1958. (Courtesy of Howard University Moorland-Spingarn Research Center)

Reception for Poet Robert Frost at Morehouse College, 30 January 1955. (Courtesy of Howard University Moorland-Spingarn Research Center)

Dr. and Mrs. Benjamin E. Mays (Sadie) entertaining students in their home. (Courtesy of Morehouse College)

Dr. Benjamin Mays at Atlanta University Board of Trustees meeting. (Courtesy of Spelman College Archives)

Dr. Mays at conference. (Courtesy of Howard University Moorland-Spingarn Research Center)

Dr. Mays with students and faculty of Morehouse College. (Courtesy of Howard University Moorland-Spingarn Research Center)

(Above) Dr. Martin Luther King, Jr., with Dr. Benjamin E. Mays at the All University Center Convocation. (Courtesy of Morehouse College Archives) (Below) Dr. David Satcher and other Morehouse Men featured with Dr. Mays. (Courtesy of Dr. David Satcher)

BENJAMIN ELIJAH MAYS

Reverend Maynard Jackson (Mayor Maynard Jackson's father), Spelman president
Florence Read. Standing: Professor G. C. Chandler and Dr. Mays. (Courtesy of
Morehouse College Archives)

Reverend Maynard Jackson, Dr. Benjamin E. Mays. Seated behind Dr. Mays is Dr. Martin Luther King, Sr. (Courtesy of Morehouse College Archives)

Dr. Benjamin E. Mays and President Tubman of Liberia, after receiving honorary degree from Morehouse College. (Courtesy of Howard University Moorland-Spingarn Research Center)

Atlanta University Center presidents: Dr. Rufus Clement, Atlanta University; Dr. W. A. Fountain, Morris Brown College; Miss Florence Read, Spelman College; Dr. Harry Richardson, Interdenominational Theological Center; Dr. Benjamin E. Mays, Morehouse College. (Courtesy of Howard University Moorland-Spingarn Research Center)

Dr. John W. Davis, Dr. Benjamin E. Mays, and Dr. Carter G. Woodson, commencement Morehouse College, 1946. (Courtesy of Howard University Moorland-Spingarn Research Center)

(Above) President Florence Read of Spelman College, actor Paul Roberson, President Rufus Clement of Atlanta University, and Dr. Benjamin E. Mays. (Courtesy of Morehouse College Archives) (Below) Dr. William Danforth, member of Morehouse College Board of Trustees, stands with President Mays before portrait of Danforth's grandfather in Dr. Mays's office. (Courtesy of Howard University Moorland-Spingarn Research Center)

Dr. Mays at ceremony in front of Danforth Chapel. (Courtesy of Morehouse College Archives)

Dr. Benjamin E. Mays featured with the Danforth family. (Courtesy of Morehouse College Archives)

Laying the cornerstone at the dedication of Danforth Chapel on Morehouse College campus. (Courtesy of Morehouse College Archive)

Dr. Benjamin E. Mays with Morehouse College trustees. (Courtesy of Morehouse College Archives)

Dean Rusk and Dr. Mays at Atlanta University. (Courtesy of Howard University Moorland-Spingarn Research Center)

President Mays with Catherine Waddell at Spelman social function, 1961. (Courtesy of Howard University Moorland-Spingarn Research Center)

Dr. Benjamin E. Mays, Francis Cardinal Spellman, and Mr. and Mrs. John D. Rockefeller, Jr. (Courtesy of Howard University Moorland-Spingarn Research Center)

Morehouse Men with Dr. Benjamin E. Mays. (Courtesy of Howard University Moorland-Spingarn Research Center)

Dr. Benjamin E. Mays attending reception at Morehouse College. (Courtesy of Morehouse College Archives)

Dr. Benjamin E. Mays autographs his book *Seeking to Be Christian in Race Relations*.
(Courtesy of Morehouse College)

Dr. Mays and Morehouse School of Religion faculty. (Courtesy of Howard University Moorland-Spingarn Research Center)

Federal Council of Churches of Christ incoming president, Bishop G. Bromsley Oxnam (1944–1946), outgoing president the Right Reverend Henry St. George Tucker, and President Benjamin E. Mays. (Courtesy of Howard University Moorland-Spingarn Research Center)

Left to right: unknown, Cardinal Spellman, Mrs. Sadie Mays, and Dr. Benjamin E. Mays.
(Courtesy of Howard University Moorland-Spingarn Research Center)

Dr. Mays, Mrs. Charles Merrill, Mrs. Sadie Mays, and Mr. Charles Merrill. (Courtesy of Howard University Moorland-Spingarn Research Center)

Hard Copy. Dr. Benjamin Mays, Miss Rhoda Jordan, Mrs. Sadie Mays and Mr. Charles Merrill. (Courtesy of Howard University Moorland-Spingarn Research Center)

Morehouse students awarded the 1964–1965 Merrill European Travel study grants based on scholarship, personality, social maturity, intellectual promise, character, and integrity: Jethro Toomer, Wililliam C. Ward, Allen Carter, Henry M. Thompson, Clarence Lawrence, and Kenneth E. Fowler. (Courtesy of Morehouse College)

1958 Merrill Travel study recipients (seated left to right): Dr. E. A. Jones, Morehouse; Dr. T. J. Jarrett, Atlanta University; Mrs. Billie Geter Thomas, Spelman College; Dr. Benjamin E. Mays, Charles E. Merrill, Jr., trustee chairman of Morehouse College; President Albert Manley, Spelman College; Dr. R. H. Brisbane, Morehouse College; Dr. Howard Zinn, Spelman College. Standing are the six Morehouse students, the two Spelman students, and the two Atlanta University students who received the Merrill Awards for 1958/59. (Courtesy of Morehouse College)

Dr. Benjamin Mays, Mr.Charles Merrilll. Mrs. Sadie Mays, and Miss Rhoda Jordan with faculty recipients of travel grants. (Courtesy of Morehouse College)

Dr. Benjamin E. Mays at a football game. (Courtesy of Morehouse College Archives)

Dr. Benjamin E. Mays and Mrs. Sadie Mays at a ceremony in 1966. (Courtesy of Spelman College Archive)

Morehouse College groundbreaking for physical education and health building at the school's ninetieth anniversary: Dr. Albert Manley, Dr. Mordecai Johnson, Dr. Mays, Dr. John H. Davis, Dr. Rufus Clement, and Coach Frank Forbes. (Courtesy of Howard University Moorland-Spingarn Research Center)

Morehouse confers the degree of Doctor of Humane Letters upon Dr. Mays, 6 June 1967. (Courtesy of Howard University Moorland-Spingarn Research Center)

Dr. Mays lights candles on Founder's Day cake, 1963. (Courtesy of Morehouse College)

At Morehouse 1967 Centennial Banquet: President Mays, Mrs. Sadie Mays, speaker Dr. Howard Thurman, Mrs. Beulah Gloster, and Dr. Hugh Gloster. (Courtesy of Howard University Moorland-Spingarn Research Center)

Dr. Mays at Second Century ceremony at Morehouse College. (Courtesy of Morehouse College)

Morehouse Centennial Convocation, June 1967: Romeo Horton, L. V. Booth, Charles Merrill, Dr. Mays, William Trent, James H. Birnie, and Roland Smith. (Courtesy of Howard University Moorland-Spingarn Research Center)

Dr. Hugh Gloster, Atlanta mayor Ivan Allen, and Dr. Mays at June 1967 banquet honoring Dr. and Mrs. Mays. (Courtesy of Howard University Moorland-Spingarn Research Center)

Mayor Ivan Allen, Jr., and Dr. Benjamin E. Mays chat at banquet.
(Courtesy of the Atlanta Journal-Constitution)

Dr. Albert Manley presenting Dr. and Mrs. Mays a gift in honor of Dr. Mays's retirement as president of Morehouse College. The gift was presented during Spelman's Commencement Convocation in Sisters Chapel, 29 May 1967. (Courtesy of Spelman College Archives)

Spelman College honors Dr. and Mrs. Benjamin E. Mays. (Courtesy of Spelman College Archives)

Mays at twentieth anniversary of President Manley of Spelman College, 1973. (Courtesy of Spelman College Archives)

BENJAMIN E. MAYS AND HIS FAMILY

John Mays, Dr. Mays's older brother. Benjamin was the youngest of eight children: Susie, Sarah, Mary, James, Isaiah, John, Hezekiah, and Benjamin. (Courtesy of Bernice Perkins)

Hezikiah Mays, Dr. Mays's older brother. (Courtesy of Bernice Perkins)

Dr. Mays, Mrs. Bernice Perkins, and other family members. (Courtesy of Bernice Perkins)

Dr. Mays on cruise ship. (Courtesy of Howard University Moorland-Spingarn Research Center)

Dr. and Mrs. Benjamin E. Mays boarding train for Egypt, 1952. (Courtesy of Howard University Moorland-Spingarn Research Center)

Dr. and Mrs. Benjamin E. Mays attending White House dinner honoring the Shah of Iran, 11 April 1962. (Courtesy of Howard University Moorland-Spingarn Research Center)

Here we are to say we were made happy, grateful and humble by the Many who remembered us As we celebrated the 25th Anniversary of our Marriage on October 14, 1951. Sincerely Yours Mr. & Mrs. B.E. Mays August 9, 1926 – August 9, 1951

Dr. and Mrs. Benjamin E. Mays at the couple's twenty-fifth wedding anniversary.
(Courtesy of Howard University Moorland-Spingarn Research Center)

Dr. and Mrs. Benjamin E. Mays. (Courtesy of Morehouse College)

Dr. Mays is featured with his niece Nettie Powell (with arms folded). (Courtesy of Howard University Moorland-Spingarn Research Center. Photograph by Jim Wells.)

Dr. Mays and Tawana Wimbish (niece) at Bates College, 1982. (Courtesy of Howard University Moorland-Spingarn Reseach Center)

Chapter 4

RETIREMENT YEARS: AN ACTIVE GIANT

"Retirement" was not a word in Dr. Mays's vocabulary. He yearned to continue serving and did so. Mays was continuously sought-after as a speaker, preacher, and lecturer.

The years 1968–1969 were demanding. While serving as a visiting professor and advisor to the president of Michigan State University, Mays also served as a consultant in 1969 for the nation's Office of Health, Education, and Welfare. During this time, his sixth book, a compilation of sermons titled *Disturbed About Man*, was published.

Dr. Mays's autobiography, *Born To Rebel*, was published in 1971. It is a penetrating study that covers almost seventy-five years of race relations in the United States.

He still wanted to give more; consequently, *Lord, The People Have Driven Me On* was published in 1981. This volume describes his early childhood on a farm in South Carolina and his educational journey that led to the presidency of Morehouse College. In it he acknowledges those people who were major sources of encouragement.

In 1983, *Quotable Quotes of Benjamin E. Mays* was published. This, his final book, represents his thoughts on education, life, race, and religion.

Between 1968 and 1983, Dr. Mays received thirty-four honorary degrees from a variety of institutions such as Michigan State University, East Lansing, Michigan; New York University, New York, New York; Middlebury College, Middlebury, Vermont; Emory University, Atlanta, Georgia; Brandeis University, Waltham, Massachusetts; Centre College of Kentucky, Danville, Kentucky; Benedict College, Columbia, South Carolina; Yeshiva University, New York, New York; University of Ife, Ile-Ife, Nigeria; Pratt Institute, New York, New York; Alderson-Broaddus College, Philippi, West Virginia; Coe College, Cedar Rapids, Iowa; Lander College, Greenwood, South Carolina; Interdenominational Theological Center, Atlanta, Georgia; Olivet College, Olivet, Michigan; Duke University, Durham, North

Carolina; Dillard University, New Orleans, Louisiana; Dartmouth College, Hanover, New Hampshire; University of South Carolina, Columbia, South Carolina; State University of New York, Old Westbury, New York; Tuskegee Institute, Tuskegee, Alabama; and Oberlin College, Oberlin, Ohio.

Mays also received numerous awards during retirement which include the Religious Leaders Award, the National Conference of Christians and Jews, Martin Luther King, Jr. Freedom Award, the Roy Wilkins NAACP Award—Scholar, Clergyman, Statesman, and Humanitarian, Hale Woodruff Award, the University of Chicago Alumni Medal, the Distinguished American Educator Award from the United States Office of Education, the Mutual of Omaha Criss Award, *Ebony* Lifetime Achievement Award, the Golden Staff Award from Georgia State University, and the Shining Light Award from WSB Radio.

Even though Dr. Mays received numerous awards, he was honored and touched when his birth state, South Carolina, inducted him into the South Carolina Hall of Fame in January 1983 and hung his portrait in the State House of the South Carolina capitol in Columbia, South Carolina.

The Atlanta Board of Education[39]

At age seventy-five, Dr. Benjamin Mays ran for a seat on the Atlanta Board of Education. He was successful in this run and later was elected the first African-American president of the board. Mays assumed this giant task while the Atlanta public schools were facing court-mandated desegregation. The case subsequently broadened from Atlanta to the larger metropolitan area, which included approximately ten school districts.

During the desegregation process, the school system started losing white teachers and white children due to a major population shift often called "white flight." However, people were moving out of the city for various reasons. Atlanta was undergoing enormous commercial growth, particularly in the predominantly white residential sections of the city. The influx of businesses into the city wiped out white communities and contributed to the rapid growth of suburban areas—growth that had started with the end of World War II.

It became obvious that the city was not going to have many white children to desegregate. As a result, the federal court pressured the city to speed up the process of submitting a plan in order to desegregate the public schools. Mays wrote in *Born to Rebel* that the "decision of the federal court that the city's public schools had to be desegregated by 1 February 1970, on a ratio of 57 percent black and 43 percent white teachers, created consternation among many white Atlantans."[40] Atlanta City Board of Education felt that it did not need to address busing because the city had never had a busing system. However, the court decision in Alabama said if it takes busing to desegregate, cities have to implement a bus system. Such an ultimatum placed a whole different equation on the Atlanta dilemma.

The Atlanta Board of Education could not agree on a plan. The attorneys then asked the court for assistance—in effect, forcing the court to delineate what it wanted. The tactic was successful; the court was responsible for bringing all of the parties together, which resulted in what became known as the Atlanta Compromise Plan.

The plan essentially followed board member Dr. Asa Yancey's recommendation to make the administration of the system "colorless." Board members agreed to begin the desegregation process at the administrative level, placing both an African American and a white at the top. The board ended up with a volunteer transportation plan. It was called "majority to minority," better known as "M to M." The plan allowed each student to transfer to any school where his or her race was in the minority, which was especially effective for the black students. The white students did not want to be bused to South Atlanta. The black students were bused to previously white schools if they wanted to go. This plan was strictly a volunteer decision and later became known as the Volunteer Transfer Program (VTP). The plan was to be monitored by the courts and the board had to give certain periodic reports to the Department of Health, Education and Welfare on how the plan was working. The plan was then given to the court where the attorneys asked that it be made an order of the court. On 28 July 1974, the Atlanta School System was declared unitary.

Mays played a pivotal role in the desegregation process as president of the board because he was held in such high esteem. His negotiating style involved seeking the opinion of each board member privately. By the force of his personality, no one—white or black—was going to do anything to dishonor Mays. In the negotiations to resolve the suit, Mays knew that the only way it was going to work would be to have the system and the board behind it. It would have been useless to implement a plan and then have everyone trying to destroy it. "If we had not had Dr. Mays as president of the Board during this period, it would have blown up and no one was going to do that because it would have brought dishonor to Dr. Mays," said attorney Warren Fortson.[41] He further commented that "the strength of the man was in his character, who he was, and the tremendous respect people had for him."[42]

Board member Ann Woodward said that "Dr. Mays's approach was the kind that was logical, non-forceful, nor insulting; therefore, everyone was willing to cooperate with him. He did not do it himself, but he was the leader and he set the stage for us."[43]

In Warren Fortson's words, "Black children missed out because of segregation, and white children missed out on the experience of knowing Dr. Benjamin Mays, the person he was and what he had to contribute. He was the classic example of what generations of white children missed out on."[44]

One of the greatest moments for Dr. Mays was the selection of Dr. Alonzo Crim as the first African-American superintendent of the Atlanta School System on 1 July 1973. Dr. Mays stood like the Colossus at Rhodes between Dr. Crim, the board, the city of Atlanta, and all other detractors. He felt that it was his duty as president of the board to allow Dr. Crim the opportunity to run the school system.

Because of the growth in southwest Atlanta, a new high school became a real need, and land was acquired on Benjamin E. Mays Drive. Formerly named Sewell Road, this street in southwest Atlanta was named in Mays's honor in August 1981. Then the board turned its attention to naming the new school. It had been the policy of the board that school buildings could not be named for someone until that person had been deceased for two years. However, board member Ann Woodward made a motion at a school board meeting that the rule be set aside. Her motion passed, and Woodward then moved that the new school be named in honor of President Benjamin E. Mays. It was passed. Dr. Mays was deeply proud of this magnet school in mathematics, and he visited it often while it was being built.

While Mays High School was being built, I chaired a committee consisting of volunteers from across the metropolitan Atlanta area under the umbrella of Collection of Life and Heritage Museum to produce an exhibit on Dr. Mays that would coincide with the opening of the school. With Dr. Mays's help, we produced an exhibit that later became popular for use by educational institutions, churches, and the Georgia capitol. The Benjamin E. Mays Archive was established at Mays High School on 10 February 1985, in order for the students to know and to learn more about the man for whom the school was named.

Atlanta is richer as a result of Mays's leadership on the school board during those difficult times. "I feel that the schools are great today because of his influence," said Ann Woodward.[45] After serving four terms spanning twelve years, Dr. Mays decided not to seek re-election and retired as a public servant in 1981.

Photo of Benjamin E. Mays entitled, "Packing Up". (Courtesy of Kenneth F. Hodges/LyBensons Gallery)

Dr. Mays receives honorary Doctor of Humanities degree from Boston University, 1950. (Courtesy of Howard University Moorland-Spingarn Research Center)

(Above) President Benjamin E. Mays, Dean John U. Monro, Leonard Bernstein, and Professor Randall Thompson at Harvard University, 15 June 1967. (Courtesy of Howard University Moorland-Spingarn Research Center) (Below) Dr. Mays received honorary Doctor of Laws degree from Harvard University, 1967. (Courtesy of Howard University Moorland-Spingarn Research Center)

Processional to commencement exercises, Harvard University, 15 June 1967. (Courtesy of Howard University Moorland-Spingarn Research Center)

Dr. Mays receives honorary Doctor of Laws degree from Michigan State, 1968.
(Courtesy of Howard University Moorland-Spingarn Research Center)

Dr. Benjamin E. Mays receives honorary degree from Dartmouth in 1975. (Courtesy of Howard University Moorland-Spingarn Research Center)

Dr. Benjamin E. Mays receives Doctor of Humane Letters degree from State University of New York, the College of Old Westbury. He is featured with Marian Wright Edelman. (Courtesy of State University of New York, the College of Old Westbury)

Dr. Arthur Fleming, Dr. Benjamin E. Mays, and Governor Jimmy Carter as Mays receives the Older Georgian Award, 7 August 1971. (Courtesy of the Atlanta Journal-Constitution)

Dr. Mays and Mayor Maynard Jackson, April 1976. (Courtesy of Howard University Moorland-Spingarn Research Center)

Mayor Maynard Jackson presents Dr. Mays with a replica of a new street sign named for him; John Sweet is in background. (Courtesy of the Atlanta Journal-Constitution)

Benjamin E. Mays, Elmo Ellis, vice president and general manager of WSB Radio, and Joe T. LaBoon, president of Atlanta Gas Light Company, pose next to the plaque honoring Dr. Mays, 1981. (Courtesy of the Atlanta Journal-Constitution) (Below) Dr. Louis W. Sullivan, president of Morehouse School of Medicine and guests at the Mays exhibit at the Morehouse School of Medicine. (Courtesy of Carrie Dumas)

Viewing the Benjamin E. Mays Exhibit at Mays High School are Jeanine Oliga, Mayor Maynard Jackson and Representative Henrietta Canty. (Courtesy of Carrie Dumas)

Dr. Mays featured with Ann Woodward at Emory University's Mays exhibit, 7 November 1982. (Courtesy of Emory University Special Collections; used by permission of Emory University)

Benjamin E. Mays with student reporter at Emory University. (Courtesy of Emory University Special Collections; used by permission of Emory University)

Dr. Benjamin E. Mays, Lelia Crawford, William Fox , and Jack Boozer. (Courtesy of Emory University Special Collections; used by permission of Emory University)

Former mayor of Atlanta Sam Massell, Dr. Benjamin E. Mays, Superintendent of Atlanta Public Schools Letson, and others. (Courtesy of Sam Massell)

Dr. Benjamin E. Mays, Superintendent of Atlanta Public Schools John Letson, and Governor Jimmy Carter. (Courtesy of Kenan Research Center at the Atlanta History Center)

Dr. Alonzo Crim and Dr. Benjamin E. Mays. (Courtesy of the Atlanta Journal-Constitution)

J. Y. Moreland, Robert Robinson, Jack Sumners, Jim Maddox, Dr. Benjamin E. Mays, John Sweet, Michael Bond, Rob Pitts, and Ann Woodward, 1982. (Courtesy of the Atlanta City Council)

Mayor Maynard H. Jackson and Dr. Benjamin E. Mays. (Courtesy of the Atlanta City Council)

Dr. Benjamin E. Mays. (Courtesy of Morehouse College Archives)

Chapter 5

LEGACY: REMEMBERING THE EDUCATOR, CLERGYMAN, WORLD-RENOWNED LEADER

DR. MAYS OFTEN SAID THAT WHAT'S IMPORTANT ISN'T HOW long we live, but how well we live and what contribution we make to mankind. He was a living example of this philosophy by the lives he touched. He left an indelible impression on many of them, such as former president Jimmy Carter, former surgeon general David Satcher, former chairman of the Morehouse College Board of Trustees, Charles Merrill, and many others. As a tribute to his legacy, statements from some of the people that Dr. Mays touched are shared below.

David Satcher, M.D., Ph.D.—director of the National Center for Primary Care, Morehouse School of Medicine; former United States surgeon general:

I came to Morehouse College in 1959 from a small farm in Anniston, Alabama. I had lived in an environment where racism and discrimination against blacks were the norm. Neither of my parents finished elementary school but they wanted their nine children to get an education and supported us through high school. I was fortunate to earn a scholarship to Morehouse College. From the moment that I met Dr. Benjamin Elijah Mays as he spoke to us as new students during my first week of matriculation, he set a standard of excellence and ethics for me. He personally symbolized the Morehouse environment of high expectations. He elevated my perception of myself as a young black man. He wanted us to know that we were special and that we were expected to be leaders. I knew that if I could make it as a "Morehouse Man" that I could make it anywhere. In short, Dr. Benjamin

Mays was a symbol of the Morehouse College's environment of support and high expectations that became a part of my experience.

Whenever and wherever Dr. Mays spoke, he provided quality, substance and inspiration in his message. He was a tremendous role model for the students of Morehouse College and especially for me. I would later become student body president in my senior year, and a leader in the Atlanta University Center's Student Nonviolent Coordinating Committee (SNCC). In these roles, I dealt directly with Dr. Mays on several occasions. I remember, once after returning to campus after spending a week in jail for sitting-in at a restaurant, Dr. Mays asked to see me. When I went to see him his concern was that we had not informed him of our planned engagement in this activity; had he known he could have called the chief of police who was a friend of his to make sure he looked out for us.

As student body president, I challenged Dr. Mays to allow a two-day reading period at the end of the semester so that students could gather their thoughts and information and, thus, perform at their best. He, in turn, after agreeing to experiment with this proposal, challenged me to prove that students would use these days for study and not for other activities. Along with the members of the student council, I was able to meet Dr. Mays's challenge and the percentage of students on the honor roll doubled in time. This became a major factor in Morehouse College qualifying for Phi Beta Kappa, which had long been a dream of Dr. Mays's.

Now fast forward to October 1982: I am being inaugurated as the eighth president of Meharry Medical College in Nashville, Tennessee. Dr. Mays, now in a wheelchair, made a powerful speech challenging me and Meharry Medical College to "aim for the ceiling and not the floor." This had been a favorite saying of his when I was a student at Morehouse College. But even today, I can still hear his voice (he died in March 1984) challenging me to excellence and to a standard of ethics worthy of the "Morehouse Man."

Over the years I have used many of Benjamin Mays's quotes, but my favorite quote of all is a special reminder of how he challenged us to new heights: "Not failure, but low aim is sin."

Bernice Mays Perkins—niece:

Dr. Benjamin Elijah Mays was to me an extraordinary, wonderful, humble man whom I loved, admired, and respected so much. He enriched my life greatly with his being, his speeches, his writings and his kindness. I still thank God for allowing me to be part of his life, and he being family. I am grateful to him for lessons taught in responsibility, trust, honesty, integrity, steadfastness, love of God, family and mankind, qualities he embodied. To me, my uncle was a prince among men.

I loved and admired his rebellious stance. In his writings and speeches, against unjust laws and social injustice, he had the courage to point out the wrongs directed toward blacks and other minorities. Dr. Mays never deviated from what was factual, never deviated from what was right, never deviated from what was just, truthful, or kind. He never left out God in his equation of his life, and he gave God the glory. What a noble life he led! What an example he left to follow! What a man and teacher he was! So precious was he, so loved was he, so missed is he.

Charles Merrill—former chairman
of the Morehouse College Board of Trustees:

Benjamin E. Mays was one of the great figures in life. He was one of the small number of genuine Christians I have ever known. He was the first black man whom I could ever call a friend, the first to open the door for me of the realities in our unhappy nation. What was it to be a teacher, an officer, a leader, perhaps, what can be the proper mixture of courtesy, forcefulness, modesty, pride, faith and realism that together lead from greatness to nobility? "I realized that God had called me to do something worthwhile in the world" was a sentence that rose within Mays from boyhood. That strength of religious faith, that very evident conviction behind his words— "the birthright of equality is given by God"—that he believed what he said, that behind his reserved courtesy was an absolute moral integrity, made it difficult for any white Southerner to push him around.

Mays would be proud that Morehouse College is still respected as America's leading black college. He would have been overjoyed by the authority that Colin Powell's sober judgment has won him as secretary of state. By the choice of black women as president of both Smith and Brown.

How distinct was this man. Yes, he was a man of integrity, good judgment, basic kindness. One felt reassured, no matter where one stood, that our country, our time, still produced a man like Benjamin Elijah Mays.

Dr. Lawrence N. Jones—dean and professor emeritus,
Howard University School of Divinity:

I met Benjamin Mays sixty-two years ago when he came to West Virginia State to speak. I was a student assistant in the president's office and was assigned to escort him around campus and so I got an opportunity to converse with him. I never in my wildest dreams thought that I would be one of his successors as dean of the then School of Religion at Howard University. When the Divinity School moved into its new home in 1987 we were proud to name it the Benjamin E. Mays Hall. Over the years, I came to know Dr. Mays more intimately and visited him in his home on several occasions. He was a wonderful storyteller, a skilled orator and preacher, a visionary administrator, an informed national and international churchman, and a dedicated public servant. I was influenced by his unique melding of his life as a scholar, educator, and administrator with that of church leader, practicing Christian, and enlightened thinker. He was a man without pretension and was unimpressed by his own celebrity and reputation. A friend to persons of all races and classes, he was a remarkable and wise man. That he was one of the distinguished leaders of the twentieth century is beyond dispute.

Jimmy Carter—former president of the United States and Nobel laureate:

Dr. Mays was a quiet and modest Christian gentleman, but at the same time a monumental figure in the fields of education and social progress. He demonstrated a standard of personal wisdom, dedication, and courage that helped to transform the social consciousness of our nation, and served to enhance our country's leadership in the international struggle for human rights. He was an inspiration to all of us who knew him.

This man of humble beginnings persistently challenged himself, and in the process provided us with greater understanding of our potential and the realization that our highest goals might be attained.

Benjamin Mays was my personal friend, my constructive critic, and my close adviser. His death was a sad day for all those who love peace and justice.

Asa G. Yancey, M.D.—
former CEO of Grady Fulton County Hospital System, Atlanta, Georgia:

Dr. Benjamin E. and Sadie G. Mays were my patients for several years. They were patients who led wholesome lives and practiced excellent health habits.

The Atlanta Board of Education, on which I served as a member, elected Dr. Mays as president with pride. Usually votes of the board are open but several members wished to register secret ballots in order not to confront their friends. The secret ballot elected Dr. Mays by a significant majority and he provided leadership for the board with distinction for many years. The Mays board of education accomplished desegregation of the Atlanta Public School System without arithmetical busing with input by the Board Desegregation Committee, chaired by Lonnie King. I was the prime desegregation litigant who fostered integration of ethnic groups without total busing. Our board purchased the land on which Mays High School now stands, and Anne Woodward proposed the name Benjamin E. Mays High School.

Dr. Mays's word was his bond and truly great was his leadership. Our board felt that a totally African-American school could perform as well as a totally European background one if all parameters were equal. Our board positively refused to allow the teaching of so-called black English.

Margaret Cyrus—administrator, Division of Educational Policy and
Administration, University of Southern California's Rossier School
of Education; former secretary to Dr. Mays:

I thank God for every remembrance of Dr. Mays. The day-to-day working relationship afforded me the opportunity to come to know the genius of this man. With compassion, he dedicated his life's work to the task of motivating and educating people from all walks of life. From where I sat, there was never a dull moment in the office. Admirable were his strength and courage.

There was an incident in January 1979 that I vividly remember, however, with tears of joy. It was a perfect "Kodak moment." Sudden snow covered the grounds; nothing would stop Dr. Mays from getting to the annual Dr. Martin Luther King, Jr.'s Birthday Observance at Ebenezer

Baptist Church. I watched him from the office window, struggling to get his car turned around for the trip into town. To no avail, the car wheels continued to spin and sputter in the snow and ice. He created an unbelievable scene, as the car came to a halt with the tail bumper smashed near the trunk of one of the tall pine trees that shaded his backyard. He returned to the house and prepared himself to leave again. I just knew he would not dare try to drive his vehicle down the sloped driveway again where sheets of ice lay underneath the snow. This time, he came through the office all handsomely wrapped. I looked at him and sternly remarked, "Where are you going?" He told me what I did not want to hear—that he was driving. Needless to say, I persuaded him to let me get the car to the street. Determination was definitely his style.

Privileged to work with Dr. Mays and in the typing of his many lecture notes, addresses, sermons, prayers, and his book, *Lord, The People Have Driven Me On*, I found out what manner of man he really was. Strength was his nature. Courage was his stature.

Mary L. Stone, Ph.D.—retired Pittsburgh public schools counselor:

I had the good fortune of meeting Dr. Benjamin E. Mays over sixty years ago when I was an undergraduate student at South Carolina State College in Orangeburg, South Carolina. When I first heard that Dr. Mays would be the speaker for our Easter services, I was disgusted because I wanted to go home for the holiday. We were not permitted to leave school when Dr. Mays came to our campus. But, when I saw him and heard his message, I was happy I had the opportunity to hear him and be in his presence.

Dr. Mays would deliver our mid-morning Easter address at White Hall. He would come in immaculately dressed in a cutaway formal daytime coat with tails and striped pants. He urged us to complete our education and try hard to be somebody. After all these years, I remember Dr. Mays as one of my heroes.

Dr. Harriett S. Walton—former professor of mathematics at Morehouse College:

Dr. Mays hired me to teach mathematics at Morehouse College, beginning in the fall of 1958. I found Dr. Mays to be one who always expected his students and faculty to be the best that they could be. He was "a man of his word" and expected us to be the same. We did not have contracts for our employment; a verbal agreement or letter sufficed.

Dr. Mays often boasted of the excellent preparation of his faculty and the percentage that held Ph.D. degrees. As I sat and listened, I always said to myself, "and I'm not one of them." So I was compelled to study for a terminal degree. With his encouragement and adequate financial support, and three children under five years of age, I enrolled in a Ph.D. program at the Georgia Institute of Technology in 1964. The time was not well chosen, and I discontinued my studies after two years. However, Dr. Mays had instilled in me the feeling that he had very high expectations for me and that he did not accept "incomplete" work. We attended the same church and we saw each other from time to time after he retired as president of the college. In the fall of 1975, now with four children, I was happy to inform him of my plans to study and he was one of the first to know when the degree was to be awarded in 1979. My dissertation was dedicated to the three male mentors who expected me to reach great heights—my father, Reverend Ester J. Junior Sr., Dr. Joseph J. Dennis (both deceased at the time), and Dr. Benjamin E. Mays. (Since each of these men had achieved "unrealistic" goals, I could not take their expectations lightly.)

Clinton E. Warner, M.D.—retired Atlanta surgeon:

It is very appropriate for Ms. Dumas to produce this collection on Dr. Mays. The words serve to illustrate the influence that Dr. Mays so brilliantly wielded, not only in the twenty-seven years as president of the College, which has influenced the thousands of young men who have passed through. His career and the influence it produced is known over the world—and continues to shape the mission of education and society. His legacy continues to shine brightly and still serves as a beacon to all. Some lives never die, the legacy continues ad infinitum.

Dr. Mays loved my wife, Sally, who served him competently during his last few years as executive secretary, and saw to it that his affairs, his funeral, and will were executed properly, as he wished. I feel that my connection was special as he and my father were close friends for decades before I was born. They were friends when both were on the faculty in 1923, and he asked my father to come back to Morehouse after he (Mays) became president. He once lost a wager to me on an Atlanta Braves game, which he loved also. He insisted on paying up, over my objections, writing a check that I immediately donated to the Sadie Mays Nursing Home. He also never suffered from "Scared Negro Disease" that seems to be afflicting most of our "leaders" currently. This disease is absolutely fatal to personal integrity.

To fight this destructive, anti-alchemic process, we must take the lessons we learned from our Morehouse transformation and unerringly apply them to our every endeavor.

Thanks to the author for covering some of those miles and strengthening and extending the legacy of Dr. Mays.

Dr. Jeannette Hume Lutton—retired professor of English, Morehouse College:

I have never known anyone who had greater influence for good. Both by his teaching (the famous chapel talks) and by his example of integrity, dignity, purpose, and strength, he was an inspiration to generations of students and, indirectly, to whose lives they touched. No one who knew him could fail to realize that he represented what we should mean when we speak of a great man.

Mrs. Charlie Henderson—friend to Dr. Mays:

Dr. Mays was a warm, charming, Christian gentleman. My husband, Butler Henderson, and I looked upon him as a friend who was loyal and true, or a big brother. After we moved to New York he always spent one week each summer for his vacation with us. Dr. Mays always signed his handwritten notes to us, "Bennie." He wanted us to call him "Bennie," but we had too much respect for him. Of course, we called him "Bennie" behind his back.

Audrey Forbes Manley—president emerita, Spelman College:

Dr. Benjamin Elijah Mays was the epitome of black manhood. His presence and person were of such dignity and regal magnitude that he defied easy description. He was essentially a holy man whose brilliance and transcendent gifts of spirit were totally committed to empowering and transforming the lives of the young black men who matriculated at Morehouse College. His reach extended beyond those campus gates, for he touched the lives of many Spelman women and shaped the historical landscape of this country and the world through the ranks of students, such as Martin Luther King, Jr. and the former mayor of Atlanta, Maynard Jackson. I was blessed and honored to call this prince of a man a mentor and friend.

Dr. Herman F. Bostick—professor of French and Spanish, Howard University:

Dr. Mays harbored a deep and vivid reverence for the human mind. He shared that reverence with the Morehouse students and faculty. Each Tuesday when he was on campus, he would speak at the 9:00 A.M. chapel service. His was not a talk but an address, sometimes bordering on a sermon. It was in these addresses that Dr. Mays impressed upon us students the importance of developing our minds to the fullest.

During our very first encounter with Dr. Mays as freshmen at Morehouse, he emphasized to us that our purpose at Morehouse was to "stretch our minds and to make our brains sweat," and sweat they did!

He would intone in his marvelous oratorical voice the words of the poet, Maltbie Babcock:

> We are not here to play, to dream, to drift;
> We have hard work to do, and loads to lift.
> Shun not the struggle, face it!
> T'is God's gift.
> Be strong, O men!

Throughout our sojourn at Morehouse as students, we would often be regaled by Dr. Mays with memorable original dicta and quotations from other sources that underscored the greatness of the well-honed human mind. He would say to us, "You are what you do with your mind, and you are what you do with your youth. It is not your environment, it is you—the quality of your minds…That will decide your future. Youth is not a time of life, it is a state of mind."

These statements were pronounced with such intensity and conviction that they became branded, in our minds and in our souls. They became the mottoes by which many of us live today.

One of the many quotations Dr. Mays shared with Morehouse students which I liked and often quote to students whom I teach today are the words of the poet, William Henley: "Were I so tall as to reach the pole or grasp the ocean at a span, / I must be measured by my soul, / The mind is the standard of the man."

Dr. Mays was convinced that by developing one's mind, one could lift his sights. He could stand tall and erect and match wits with any other person irrespective of race, social status, color, or creed. He would remind us: "The man who out thinks you, rules you."

Dr. Mays, himself, was gifted with an exceptional mind, and during his youth he seized every opportunity to develop it maximally. It was the quest to develop his mental faculties that led him from the fields of Epworth, South Carolina (his birthplace), to Bates College in Lewiston, Maine, where he became an outstanding student and debater, to the University of Chicago where he earned the Doctor of Philosophy Degree and to membership in Phi Beta Kappa, America's preeminent honor society.

Dr. Mays did not devise the popular UNCF slogan, "A mind is a terrible thing to waste," but he could have since it expresses so succinctly his idea of the importance of the human mind. During his many years as president of Morehouse College he preached that message to us students with great passion and power. We believed him then and some of us are still guided by his spirit and words today.

As we face the unpredictable future, we do so in the faith that our objectives are sound, that our means of achieving them are practicable, and that man and God will assist us all the way.

Dr. Walter E. Massey, president, Morehouse College:

People often describe an outstanding leader as being larger than life, meaning that the whole of a person, one's entire presence and persona, is greater than the sum of the intellectual, physical, and spiritual parts of which he or she is made.

That is how Benjamin Elijah Mays first appeared to me—larger than life. As a young, early admissions freshman at Morehouse College in 1954, I was deeply impressed and greatly inspired by this dignified educator who led the nation's premier institution of higher education for black men. Dr. Mays had only one message for his students: You can be excellent. And, he had only one way of communicating that message: a quiet, consistent refusal to allow us to believe anything else.

I am grateful to be among the thousands of Morehouse men who continue to benefit from Dr. Mays's vision and influence. As the College's present president, I believe Dr. Mays would be proud to see that the commitment to excellence he helped to instill in me lives on in my own vision for Morehouse, that it will be among the finest liberal arts colleges in the nation—period.

There are many more voices that could be heard and their statements written here. They would describe the "work of the man" and the legacy they have received from the life and times of Benjamin E. Mays. He was truly an inspiration to the men of Morehouse, to those whose lives were touched by him in all walks of life and to the many, many children who idolized him. The respect was overflowing and empowering.

Chapter 6

SOUTH CAROLINA STATE UNIVERSITY

ONE OF DR. MAYS'S MAJOR CONNECTIONS TO HIS HOME state of South Carolina was as a distinguished alumnus of the high school department of State Agricultural and Mechanical College (later named South Carolina State University) in Orangeburg, South Carolina, and as the institution's Easter Sunday speaker. Mrs. Lucille Jewel, who was director of the Young Men's and Young Women's Christian Association activities on the campus, recommended in 1936 to the YM and YWCA that they invite one speaker and make the Easter services a statewide activity.[46]

Dr. Mays continued to serve as *the* Easter Sunday speaker for thirty-one years and frequently spoke to overflowing crowds. This was one of the highlights of the school's religious programs and the state's black community because his thought-provoking sermons left lasting impressions on the listeners.

One of his early sermons was "A Faith That Conquers." "He said that Jesus had a faith that conquered. He believed in God, the Father, but where he got in trouble was when he believed in man." Dr. Mays further stated that "the world of tomorrow will not be built by skeptics, but by people who, like Jesus, will serve God, not out of fear, nor in hope of reward, but because they love God, and believe in mankind."[47]

In his 1941 Easter sermon, Dr. Mays delivered a message of hope for humankind whom he asserted "was recalcitrant and stubborn by nature, and had almost lost his identity with God by trying to be God." Dr. Mays also declared during his discourse "that man by nature was fundamentally evil as well as fundamentally good." The view that man is fundamentally evil was unorthodox, he declared, "but was a fact supported by overwhelming evidence of man's exploitation and greed for power." He further explained, "the relationship between God and man must be mutual. Man cannot get along with God, and God cannot leave man alone. In this relationship lies hope for man which will bring ultimate peace."[48]

In his nineteenth Easter message, Dr. Mays spoke of Gethsemane. He stated that some of us will face Gethsemane through human ills, insanity, suicide, defeat, or victory and it is up to us to decide how we face it. In this message Dr. Mays spoke of his darkest hours as a child on a farm in Epworth, South Carolina. "There he literally cried for an education, and with the help of God he was able to come here to school, but even after he was here there were times when he didn't have food or clothing because his parents could not afford them. But as he said in his message 'people cling to life, it makes no difference how rocky the road, how thorny the path, they cling to life.'"[49]

In his twenty-sixth Easter message, Dr. Mays spoke of "The Real Meaning of Easter." *The Collegian: State Agricultural and Mechanical College* described the sermon this way: "He asserted that Easter is truly a thing of the heart. He further noted that it should mean more than a new dress or a new hat. Easter should not be forgotten after the Easter message is over, but it should live on throughout the year."[50]

In 1969, Dr. Mays delivered the school's Founder's Day address. He said, "There is no substitute for academic excellence, well trained, disciplined minds and skilled personnel." Mays further asserted, "You cannot black power yourself to a good job. There is no substitute for a mind that is well trained."[51]

Although written and delivered over a period of three decades, these compelling sermons are still relevant today.

Benjamin E. Mays, 1926. (Courtesy of South Carolina State University Historical
Collection)

South Carolina State, Orangebury SC, Easter service, 9 April 1939. Standing (L to R): Lillian Howard Waring, Sylvia Gilliam, Johnnie Barnes Nelson, Lottye Washington, Carolyn Durrage, Cecil Whittaker Boykin. Seated (L to R): Amanda Roundtree and Dean Thelma Chisholm Dugas. Center: Dr. Benjamin E. Mays. (Courtesy of South Carolina State University Historical Collection)

South Carolina State College 1956 Easter worship service: President B. C. Turner, Mr.
Joe Montgomery, President Mays, Miss Barbara Chandler, and Mr. Douglas L. Johnson.
(Courtesy of the South Carolina State Historical Collection)

Standing: President Benner C. Turner and Dr. Benjamin E. Mays. Seated: Mrs. Benner C. Turner, Mrs. Marian B. Wilkinson (founder of the YWCA at State College), and Mrs. Sadie Mays, Easter 1951. (Courtesy of the South Carolina State University Historical Collection)

Dr. Benjamin E. Mays, Mrs. Carrie S. Harley (former president of the State College YWCA), Miss Paula Jewel, Mrs. Katherine Chippey (director of the Student Christian Center), and Mrs. Jewel, 1961. (Courtesy of the South Carolina State University Historical Center)

THIS SCHOLAR, CLERGYMAN, EDUCATOR, AUTHOR, AND PUBLIC servant proved that he could achieve and match his mind with northern whites in spite of the era and condition into which he was born. However, because of Dr. Mays's brilliant mind and his propensity to achieve, achieve he did. Dr. Mays's faith in God was unwavering.

The treasury of pictures in this book reflects Dr. Mays's international influence during his illustrious career as a clergyman, educator, author, and public servant. His contributions to society spanned many decades and those whom he touched will carry his legacy into many generations to come.

One of Dr. Mays's greatest legacies can be summed up in his oft-quoted words, "low aim is sin." This ideal was published in *Quotable Quotes of Benjamin E. Mays*: "It must be borne in mind that the tragedy of life doesn't lie in not reaching your goal. The tragedy lies in having no goal to reach. It isn't a calamity to die with dreams unfulfilled, but it is a calamity not to dream. It is not a disaster to be unable to capture your ideal, but it is a disaster to have no ideal to capture. It is not a disgrace not to reach the stars, but it is a disgrace to have no stars to reach for. Not failure, but low aim is sin."[52]

ADDITIONAL PHOTOGRAPHS

(Above) Dr. Mays delivering eulogy at Martin Luther King, Jr.'s funeral in 1968. (Courtesy of Howard University Moorland-Spingarn Research Center) (Below) Dr. Benjamin E. Mays and Dr. Martin Luther King, Sr. (Courtesy of Mrs. Sally Warner)

Attorney Donald Hollowell, attorney Horace Ward and Dr. Benjamin E. Mays. (Courtesy of Kenneth F. Hodges/LyBensons Gallery)

Dr. Mays and Dr. Mary McLeod Bethune. (Courtesy of Howard University Moorland-Spingarn Research Center)

Dr. Benjamin E. Mays at Bennett College, Greensboro NC. (Courtesy of Howard University Moorland-Spingarn Research Center)

Processional participants at the Federal Council of the Churches of Christ in America biennial meeting, Pittsburgh PA, 28–30 November 1944. (Courtesy of Howard University Moorland-Spingarn Research Center)

Dr. Mays greeting guest. (Courtesy of Howard University Moorland-Spingarn Research Center)

Dr. Jerome H. Holland, Secretary of Labor Arthur Goldberg, and Dr. Benjamin E. Mays, 1962. (Courtesy of Howard University Moorland-Spingarn Research Center)

Mays featured with Vice President Lyndon B. Johnson attending the state funeral of Pope John XXIII, 16 June 1963. (Courtesy of Morehouse College)

Vice President Lyndon B. Johnson headed the US delegation to the Solemn Requiem Mass for Pope John XXIII in St. Peter's Basilica, Vatican City on 17 June 1963. Featured are Paul Marcinkus, the Honorable James A. Farley, Dr. George N. Shuster, and Dr. Benjamin E. Mays. (Courtesy of Howard University Moorland-Spingarn Research Center)

Dr. Mays with Crockett upon arrival in Washington, DC, at Andrews Air Force Base.
(Courtesy of Howard University Moorland-Spingarn Research Center)

Dr. Benjamin E. Mays and Sargent Shriver. (Courtesy of Howard University Moorland-Spingarn Research Center)

Secretary of State Muskie's meeting with black american leaders, 10 September 1980. Featured are Cheryl Southerland, John Touchstone, Dr. Benjamin E. Mays, Cornelius Casey, and Thomas Williams. (Courtesy of Howard University Moorland-Spingarn Research Center)

Merle H. Miller, Senator John F. Kennedy and President Benjamin E. Mays, 12 April 1959. (Courtesy of the Indianapolis Star and photographer Bob Doeppers)

At the White House with President John Fitzgerald Kennedy, 21 February 1962. Featured are President Luther H. Foster, Jr., Tuskegee Institute; President Benjamin E. Mays, Morehouse College; UNCF Executive Secretary William H. Trent, Jr.; and President Albert W. Dent, Dillard University. (Public Domain/Photographer: Cecil Stoughton)

Dr. Mays with Senator Winston Prouty (Vermont), Senator Joseph Clark (Pennsylvania), and Senator Gaylord Nelson (Wisconsin). Dr. Mays testified before the senate on hunger and malnutritionin the United States.. (Courtesy of Howard University Moorland-Spingarn Research Center)

Dr. Mays and Governor Carl E. Sanders of Georgia. (Courtesy of Howard University Moorland-Spingarn Research Center)

Dr. Mays with President Richard Nixon and others. (Courtesy of Howard University Moorland-Spingarn Research Center)

Dr. Benjamin E. Mays is greeted by Governor George Busbee. (Courtesy of the Atlanta Journal-Constitution)

Mrs. Sally Warner, Dr. Hugh Gloster, Carrie Dumas, Secretary of State David Poythress, and Dr. Benjamin E. Mays (seated), February 1982. (Courtesy of the Office of the Secretary of State David Poythress)

Senator Herman Talmadge, Clayton R. Yates, William Fowlkes, and Dr. Benjamin E. Mays. (Courtesy of Skip Mason's Archives)

President Jimmy Carter and Dr. Benjamin E. Mays. (Courtesy of Mrs. Sally Warner)

South Carolina governor Dick Riley and Dr. Mays, 1983. (Courtesy of Howard University Moorland-Spingarn Research Center)

Central Committee of the World Council of Churches in Toronto, Canada, 1950.
(Courtesy of Howard University Moorland-Spingarn Research Center)

President Mays is shown standing in front of the $450,000 consolidated school that bears his name. With him is the school's principal, Professor E. W. Brown. The school was dedicated on 9 May 1954. (Courtesy of Howard University Moorland-Spingarn Research Center)

Dr. Mays officiating at a wedding. (Courtesy of Skip Mason's archives)

Hank Aaron and Dr. Benjamin Mays at UNCF Night at Atlanta Stadium, 26 October 1967.
(Courtesy of Howard University Moorland-Spingarn Research Center)

Carrie Dumas and Mrs. Agnes Watson wish Dr. Mays well, 2 August 1977. (Courtesy of the Atlanta Journal-Constitution)

Dr. Samuel DuBois Cook and Dr. Benjamin E. Mays. (Courtesy of Mrs. Sally Warner)

Carrie Dumas and Dr. Benjamin E. Mays. (Courtesy of Mrs. Sally Warner)

Emma Hughes Business College honors Dr. Benjamin E. Mays, 17 May 1959. (Courtesy of Howard University Moorland-Spingarn Research Center)

Dr. Mays at Church of the Redeemer, spring 1968. (Courtesy of Howard University Moorland-Spingarn Research Center)

Raymond Malone II, Dr. Benjamin E. Mays, and Jamo Kenyetta Malone, 20 July 1982. Dr. Mays left the rocking chair to the author. (Courtesy of Howard University Moorland-Spingarn Research Center)

Dr. Benjamin E. Mays at a press conference. (Courtesy of the Atlanta Journal-Constitution)

Curtis Briscoe, Dr. Benjamin E. Mays, and Carrie Dumas. (Courtesy of the Atlanta Journal-Constitution)

(Left) Benjamin E. Mays. (Courtesy of Howard University Moorland-Spingarn Research Center) (Right) Benjamin E. Mays. (Courtesy of Howard University Moorland-Spingarn Research Center)

Dr. Benjamin E. Mays. (Courtesy of Howard University Moorland-Spingarn Research Center)

Dr. Benjamin E. Mays. (Courtesy of Howard University Moorland-Spingarn Research Center)

Dr. Benjamin E. Mays. (Courtesy of Howard University Moorland-Spingarn Research Center)

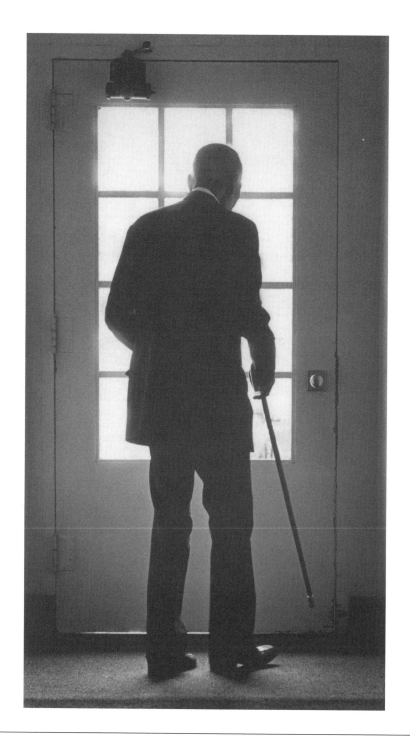

Dr. Benjamin E. Mays exiting building. (Courtesy of the Atlanta Journal-Constitution)

[1] Benjamin E. Mays, *Disturbed About Man* (Richmond VA: John Knox Press, 1969) 78.

[2] Ibid., 78.

[3] Ibid., 69.

[4] Taken from the song "Lift Every Voice and Sing" by James Weldon Johnson.

[5] *The Negro in American Life and Thought: The Nadir 1877–1907* (New York NY: Collier Books, 1954).

[6] Lerone Bennett, Jr., "The Last of the Great Schoolmasters," *Ebony*, December 1977, 77.

[7] Ibid.

[8] Marian Wright Edelman, *Lanterns: A Memoir of Mentors* (Boston: Beacon Press, 1999) 28.

[9] Bates College, "Visiting Professorship Honors Benjamin E. Mays '20," news release, December 2001.

[10] Ibid.

[11] Benjamin E. Mays, *Born to Rebel* (New York: Scribner's Sons, 1971) 36.

[12] Ibid., 35.

[13] Donald W. Harward, "Benjamin E. Mays: Legacy and Liberal Learning" (lecture, University of South Carolina, Columbia SC, 30 April 1997), Bates College Public Relations Dept.

[14] Mays, *Born to Rebel*, 67.

[15] Ibid., 97.

[16] Harward, "Benjamin E. Mays: Legacy and Liberal Learning."

[17] Mays's character always played an important role in his decisions. When he was offered the position at Howard, he had already accepted a position at another institution. With a deep sense of integrity, he decided to have a face-to-face meeting with the president of the other institution to discuss the feasibility of reversing his decision in order to provide an opportunity for him to accept the offer made by President Johnson.

[18] Mays, *Born to Rebel*, 145.

[19] Walter Dyson, *The Capstone of Negro Education* (Washington DC: Howard University, 1941) 186. In its history, Howard University School of Religion has graduated thousands of men and women, many of whom hold prominent positions within the church. Some of whom are: the late James Farmer (B.D., '41), founder of the Congress of Racial Equality and leader of the Civil Rights Movement; Rev. Young Ro An (D.Min., '98), pastor for one of Korea's leading Presbyterian congregations and advisor to the President of the Republic of South Korea; Rev. L. Vencheal Booth (B.D., '43), founded the Progressive National Baptist Convention; Bishop George Edward Battle, Jr. (D.Min.,'90), 84th bishop of the AME Zion Church; Rev. Dr. Delores Carpenter (M.Div., '69), pastor of Michigan Park Christian Church in Washington, DC, editor of the African Heritage Hymnal, and Professor of Christian Education at Howard University School of Divinity; and Rev. Dr. Vashti McKenzie (M.Div., '85), the first female Bishop in the African Methodist Episcopal Church, the nation's oldest Black denomination.

[20] Dr. Benjamin Elijah Mays and Dr. Howard Thurman, bibliography prepared for the dedication of the Benjamin E. Mays Hall and the Howard Thurman Chapel, Howard University School of Divinity, April 1987.

[21] Leonard Ray Teel, "Benjamin Mays Teaching by Example, Leading through Will," *Change Magazine*, October 1982, 21.

[22] Dr. Mays was quoted verbatim. Benjamin Mays, "Twenty-Seven Years of Success and Failure at Morehouse," *Morehouse College Bulletin*, Summer 1967, 29.

[23] Benjamin Mays, "Commencement Address: Twenty-seven Years of Success and Failure at Morehouse," *Morehouse College Bulletin*, Summer 1967, 29.

[24] Teel, "Benjamin Mays Teaching by Example, Leading through Will," 21.

[25] Ibid.

[26] Mays, "Twenty-seven Years of Success," 29.

[27] "Mays, Benjamin Elijah," in vol. 22 of *Current Biography*, ed. Anna Roth and Helen Demarest, H. W. Wilson Company, New York NY, May 1945, 392.

[28] Mays, "Commencement Address: Twenty-seven Years of Success and Failure at Morehouse," 30.

[29] The Morehouse Mystique concept grew out of Dr. Mays's ability and experience to reach for excellence, integrity, competence and high aspirations, and when students finished Morehouse they had an aura of confidence and a love for their fellowman. This phrase grew out of Mays's era as president of Morehouse.

[30] Ibid.

[31] Ibid.

[32] Noel C. Burtenshaw, "Mays Planted Seeds of Revolution in Chapel at Morehouse," *Atlanta Journal Constitution*, 1 April 1984, 8B.

[33] Mays, *Born to Rebel*, 191.

[34] Clinton E. Warner, interview by Carrie Dumas, 16–22 July 2004, Atlanta GA. (Dr. Warner was a member of the freshman class during Dr. Mays's first year as president of Morehouse College.)

[35] Anonymous, "News of the College," *Morehouse College Bulletin*, July 1958, 17.

[36] Some of the earlier student recipients of the Merrill Travel Study Award were the following: William Guy, Wilbur T. Leaphart, Morris Dillard, Donald Williams, Melvin A. Butler, James W. Patterson, A.D. Hammonds, Williams Glass, Brinston Collins, Donald R. Hopkins, Homer L. McCall, Robert H. McMillian, Benjamin D. Berry, Leroy Wilson, Joseph Rodgers, Ashton Ward, Allen C. Carter, Kenneth E. Fowler, Clarence Lawrence, Henry M. Thompson, Jethro W. Toomer, Jr., William C. Ward, John O. Hodges, Frederic G. Ransom, Robert L. Ross, Willie F. Vann, Leroy W. Vaughn, Benjamin F. Ward, Jr., James E. McLeod, Ernest L. Murphy, Carl L. Brigety, Albert H. Neal, Benjamin Daise, James C. Jones, Julius Coles, Rudolph B. Jones, William E. King, Glover Lee, William D. Robinson, Durant Worthy and many more. Some faculty who were honored to be Merrill recipients were: Professor and Mrs. G. Murray Branch, Mr. and Mrs. William M. Nix, Dr. and Mrs. Edward B. Williams, Professor and Mrs. A. Russell Brooks, Dean and Mrs. B. R. Brazeal, Dr. and Mrs. Robert H. Brisbane, Professor and Mrs. G. Lewis Chandler, Dr. and Mrs. H. C. Hamilton, Professor and Mrs. W. R. Chivers, Professor Ralph Chinn, Mrs. Jessie Ebanks, Professor Elnora Chesterman, and Professor Gerado M. Ebanks.

[37] Burtenshaw, "Mays Planted Seeds of Revolution in Chapel at Morehouse," 8B.

[38] Charlie Moreland, interview by Carrie Dumas, 17 July 2004, Atlanta GA. (Mr. Moreland was a student during Dr. Mays's administration at Morehouse College.)

[39] The contents of this section are based on an interview with retired school board attorney Warren Fortson.

[40] Mays, *Born to Rebel*, 298.

[41] Warren Forston, interview by Carrie Dumas, 18 March, 3–6 April 2004, Atlanta GA.

[42] Ibid.

[43] Ann Woodward, former Atlanta Board member, interview by Carrie Dumas, 24 February 2003, Atlanta GA.

[44] Forston, interview, 18 March, 3–6 April 2004.

[45] Woodward, interview, 24 February 2003.

[46] Benjamin E. Mays, *Lord, the People Have Driven Me On* (New York: Vantage Press, 1981) 74.

[47] Cecil Whittaker, "YW and YMCA Present Benjamin E. Mays," *The Collegian: State Agricultural and Mechanical College* 17 (1939): 1.

[48] H. Wilson, "Dr. Mays Speaks at Easter Service," *The Collegian: State Agricultural and Mechanical College* 20 (1941): 2.

[49] "Mays Delivers 19th Annual Easter Message," *The Collegian: State Agricultural and Mechanical College* 34 (1955): 7.

[50] "Dr. B. E. Mays Delivers Annual Easter Message," *The Collegian: State Agricultural and Mechanical College* 41 (1962): 1.

[51] "Skill, Training Best Route to Success—Mays," *The Collegian: State Agricultural and Mechanical College* 48 (1969): 1.

[52] Mays, *Quotable Quotes of Benjamin E. Mays*, 3.